Nature
with
Human Nature

Tanisha L. Herrin

ISBN 978-0-578-01077-9

© 2009 Tanisha L. Herrin

Dedication

During my past I have felt pain, suffering, and gone through many struggles.
This book has allowed me to see how much I have grown as an individual.
I never thought I would have done a project such as this in life.
This book is in dedication to me, myself, and I.

Contents

Best of: Book 1
Inspire the Heart, Inspire the Mind, Inspire the Spirit

- Inspiration can be… 10
- Admire 12
- Endure 14
- Rejoice 16
- Thoughts of an Evening Stroll 18
- I Am 20
- Diligence 22
- Fulfillment 24
- Gratitude 26
- Focus 28
- Determination 30
- What's Happened to Me? 32
- Wisdom 34
- Triumph 36
- You 37
- The Comforts of Home 40
- Living in the Moment 41
- Beauty of Nature in the Spring 44
- Hope 46
- Spiritual 47

Contents

Best of: Book 3
In Memory of Nancy

- I Remember When   49
- For You I Will   51
- This Isn't Goodbye   53
- N.A.N.C.Y   55
- This never came across my mind   57
- November 2nd 2005   59
- Some days   63
- Your grandson Willie   65
- The Root of my Sadness   67
- So what's next?   69
- Now Showing: The One Woman Show   71
- The Emotion of the Year   73
- Starting to slip away   75
- Cleaning Out Moms House   77
- Holding On   79
- That's Kind of Spooky   81
- July 28th 1982   83
- A Loving Memory Keepsake   85
- Simply saying thanks   87

Contents

Best of: Book 2
Trials and Tribulations of Depression:
Haiku, Quotes, and Thoughts of the Soul

-Untitled Haiku poetry   89

Additional Contents
New Featured Poetry

-Why do I?   99

-Mirror, Mirror   101

-Funny is to Laugh   103

-Road Rage   105

-Sunny Days   107

-Happy One Minute, Crabby the Next   109

-Understanding   111

-A Rainy Day   113

-A Jungle   115

-Who are you dad?   117

-Haunted Nightmare   119

-Hang in There   121

Poetry and Photography
by
Tanisha L. Herrin

www.therrinpoetry.com

7

Best of Book 1:

Inspire the Heart,
Inspire the Mind,
Inspire the Spirit.

9

Inspiration can be…

A collection of thoughts

Thoughts interpreted into actions

Actions being seen through words

Words that show different emotions

Emotions that can show feelings

Feelings that we have felt and shared

Shared with loved ones and those who have touched us

Touched us in someway, good or bad inside our hearts

Hearts in good spirits or that have been torn and repaired

Repaired by words of creative thoughtfulness

Thoughtfulness that comes from deep within

Within the body, mind, and soul

Admire

Positive characteristics that stand out effortlessly.

Admire is to wonder.
Qualities about you stay in my mind.

I applaud you when you stand up for yourself

I commend your efforts when things don't always go your way

I idolize you for showing true strength

I praise you as you have a way of helping and giving to others

I adore your funny personality

I appreciate your kind, encouraging words

I hold dearly the moments when you made me feel good about myself

I respect you for being original, just for being yourself

Endure

To take on pain of any kind.

The capacity to endure hardship or pain

Times where it's difficult to explain

Thoughts come quickly like a freight train

Thinking to break under the strain

Is like being a weak link in a chain

But I must sustain

Behind my smile I hide my pain

To come this far and still remain

Brave, strong, and fears overcame

Now memories remain

For a moment there you thought you might go insane

To come out on top with victory as your claim

Celebrate anyway you wish, maybe with Champagne

Rejoice

A time for celebration

Raise a glass and propose a toast

Enjoy times you come together with others

Joyfulness felt throughout the atmosphere

Outpour of support and praise

Involve those who are close to you

Celebrate events and special moments in life

Express emotions of happiness and delight

Thoughts of an evening stroll

I was accompanied by
memories of my childhood
last night while walking down
an old and familiar road,
As my mind wandered into
the star lit sky with a chill in the air,
I have come down this road many times before,
Looking around everything from
homes to trees look the same, but
Why do I have the sense that something has changed?
Then I remember, for so long
I used to walk this road with someone
who is no longer here, a special someone
who change the way I look at things when
they left and went to a better place,
Maybe I walked into a comfort zone
that made me feel warm and relaxed,
Or maybe it's that special someone
letting me know they are still with me,
that now I may be walking in silence, but not alone.

I Am

I am a person of wisdom
I am a person of faith
I am a person of strength
I am a person of confidence

I am a mother
I am a daughter
I am a granddaughter
I am a niece

I am intelligent
I am ambitious
I am sophisticated
I am humble

I am thoughtful
I am caring
I am humorous
I am grateful

I am quiet
I am warmhearted
I am hopeful
I am blessed

Diligence

A reflection of perfection.

An alertness that keeps you on your feet

A keenness that's deep and concrete

To adhere to a course of action or belief

A watchfulness that's not kept brief.

Energy and effort that's put in

Sincerity from underneath your own skin

Persistence through hard work that comes from within

Attention that's centered, fenced-in

Fulfillment

To fulfill a dream.

Working hard to seek a dream
May not be easy as it may seem

To help you do the best you can
Carry out a master plan

When reaching toward a goal
You are in control

If things don't work out
Try not to stress out

Something you've wanted for so long
May take time to get when things go wrong

Know what you've got to do to achieve
All you have to do is believe

A sigh of relief when things are complete
Success, a smell that is sweet

Feeling good that everything's done
A victory accomplished, a job well done

Gratitude

Thank you for everything.

all because of you
I'm eternally grateful
for what you have done

Focus

Concentrating on what is important.

Ideas of the mind

Influence and stimulate

A positive attitude

That can motivate

Oneself to stay grounded

And concentrate

Going head on with confidence

No self-hate

With no time to stop,

Look back or hesitate

Be sharp on your feet and

Don't underestimate yourself

Just keep moving

Forward and straight

Don't let anyone put you

Down or intimidate

Your actions that make

You feel just great

Determination

Willing to do whatever it takes.

Dominance in leadership

Enduring hardships that come your way

Toughness is your strength

Efforts that are endless

Resolving problems that arise

Moving at a steady pace

Intensity drives you

No is unacceptable

Assiduity always present

Tirelessness that's invisible

Intentions to come out on top

Optimism is of the essence

Never say never

Life is about good times and bad, ups and downs, and everything in between.
Sometimes so many things happen at one time you begin to struggle and
wonder when will things change and get better.
Even though we may feel weak during our struggles, from what we learn,
in the end, they make us stronger.

What's Happened to Me?

I feel like I can't go on any longer
Wondering how much more I can bare
Feeling trapped with no way out,
I'm tired of being tired yet I keep wondering
Where do I find the strength to move on?

I know I'm not perfect and things happen in life that
you have to deal with, but sometimes there are things
that hit you all of the sudden, all at once and you wonder,
What did I do to deserve this? Why is this happening?
Things happen so quickly nowadays
that it seems impossible to comprehend…

I feel scared to move on
But why? Is it because I don't know what is going to happen?
In fear of the worst happening? Who knows?
I have to move forward. It's going to get worst before it gets better.
Yet there are times the situation is so bad it's hard to even say
It will get better, that things will change…

I'm so stressed and depressed I feel like I'm not the same person anymore.
I can't think straight; it's difficult to concentrate on my work and things at home.
So many emotions running through my mind like a freight train,
Anger, sadness, emptiness, frustration, but happiness is not to be found.
At the end of the day I feel drained and hopeless…

I know things will change and get better; it's hard to be patient.
I feel like I have gone crazy and completely lost my mind!
There are so many things I have tried. Am I trying too hard?
Or hardly trying at all? I feel like I have lost myself.
I would look back and say, "I could handle this," yet it's different now…

I know you can't always look back or dwell on the past,
But I can't help it. You tend to see the good qualities about yourself
that you didn't notice before but now I don't feel the same…

As I patiently wait for relief, I'm amazed at how so many things
can change one person in such a short period of time.
One day I will be able to sleep, eat, and take care of myself the way I should.
It's like looking into the mirror where you would expect to see your reflection
but instead see someone else. The first question that comes to mind is:

What's happened to me?

Wisdom

Lessons learned are lessons shared.

Watchfulness is quiet and discreet

Intelligence a helpful tool to others

Sophistication impressive and enticing

Dexterity catches the eyes

Open-mindedness stimulates the mind

Maturity a strong sign of independence

Triumph

To come out on top is what it's all about.

Working hard to seek

a special prize

You've wanted so long

you fantasize

When the moment comes

it's no surprise

After what you've gone

through you realize

The sacrifices put

in emphasize

Hard work and persistence

that exercise

Your mind and skill

you utilize

<u>You</u>

There's no one in the world like you.

You have your own voice,
A way to express yourself

You have your own dream,
And plans to make them come true

You have you own style,
A personal look that looks good on you

You have your own personality,
That makes you different from everyone else

You have your strengths and weakness,
That makes you special in your own way

You have your own way of living,
That suits you just fine
You have your own opinions,

Other people may or may not agree

You have you own vision of the world around you,
Certain sights excite people more than others

You have your own thoughts about your future,
Where you want to go and how to get there

You have your own way of having fun,
Doing anything you want when you want to

You have you own way of solving problems,
Either trying to find a short cut or not wanting to bother at all

You have your own way of showing you care for others,
A way you make people feel special and secure

You have your own way of describing yourself,
Letting others know who you are and what your known for

You have your own way of sharing lessons,
What you've learned and how to share it with others
You know what makes you happy,
So you'll do what ever it takes so that you are

You have your own way of dealing with frustration,
Trying to sort through it or taking it out on others

You have your own way of spending time with friends,
Either you hang out a lot or just hang out by yourself

You have your own way of sharing your feelings,
Who you talk to most and what you like to talk about

You have your own way of grieving the loss of a loved one,
Some will need more time than others

You have your own way of learning about yourself,
Through your likes and dislikes

You have your own way of relaxing,
A getaway of some sort with family or a place to hide to be alone

You have you own way of what life means to you,
How you see it and how it's important.

The Comforts of Home

Time to collect yourself....
When taking care of others remember to always take care of yourself.
One way is to pamper yourself with the comforts of home.

It's just one of those days where things
around the house such as chores and
cleaning can wait just a little bit longer…

To help clear your mind
after a long day of work,
the first thing that comes to
mind are the comforts of home,

Sitting down in cozy and comfy chair
to read a good book,
Stretching out on the couch to
watch your favorite program,
Maybe you want to rest your eyes
and take a brief cat nap,

Having a cup of coffee or tea
or anything that's got a nice kick to it,
A worked up appetite for a home cooked meal,
Or take the evening off from cooking and
enjoy some delicious take out food

Spending quality time with loved ones or friends,
Listening to your favorite music
something light and mellow,
A long soothing and relaxing soak in the tub

Yet the most comfortable one of all,
the most anticipated moment at the end of the day
is to let your mind and body rest,
You slip under the covers into bed and
drift off to sleep

Living in the Moment

Living in the moment of new baby being born,
To see them open their eyes for the first time and
light up with a little smile

Living in the moment of a birthday celebration,
Stories that reminisce the special day you came
into the world and of course lets not forget about the presents!

Living in the moment of a school graduation,
Crowds cheering, clapping, and shouting
A time overwhelmed with excitement and emotions

Living in the moment of meeting a new love,
Discovering and learning things about each other that
intrigue one another leave you wanting to know more

Living in the moment of a romantic wedding,
To see a beautiful bride side by side with her groom
The moment when they begin to live together as husband and wife

Living in the moment of moving into a new home,
New space that will create new memories and
new experiences to share with others

Living in the moment of getting a new car,
The well known new car smell and the
I just can't wait to get on the road feeling

Living in the moment of a holiday celebration,
Having good food and drinks with others in
a comfortable atmosphere

Living in the moment of welcoming someone home,
They have been away awhile working hard for their families,
To see their face and know they made it home okay

Living in the moment of a couple celebrating an anniversary,
Remembering when they first met and knowing
why they have been together for as long as they have

Living in the moment of the start of retirement,
For years you have anticipated this moment and now
you have plenty of free time to do whatever your heart desires

Living in the moment of relaxation on vacation,
Your main focus is to clear your mind and
enjoy yourself as much as possible

Living in the moment of overcoming your fear,
It brings a good feeling and boosts your confidence,
at the same time your glad its over and you can move on

Living in the moment of a loss of loved one,
To look back at the last time you saw them alive
and know they were precious and close to you

Living in the moment when you look back at
what you've done in life, you have done so much and
met so many people, your adventure was like no other.

*Nature is pure and subtle in its own way.
Besides a special person who may hold strong qualities that inspire, nature has the same affect. The sights, sounds, and scents of nature can be very inspiring and uplifting to oneself. Inspirations from nature can come anytime during the year.
There's something to enjoy for everyone.*

Beauty of Nature in the Spring

Nature tends to renew itself at this time of year
Flowers blooming, petals are soft and full of color,
Smelling fresh flowers and the tickle they bring to your nose,
Watching them dance in the wind in a field,

Lakes and streams that froze from the winter cold,
Awake and thaw, begin to flow freely,
As waves flutter and glide across the water,
Little ducks playing and splashing about,

Thundershowers bathe the trees and grass,
Lightning bolts flash, racing across the sky,
Sounds of heavy rain and thunder- calming and relaxing,
Air is crisp and cool- the scent of spring rain,

The sun nourishes all living things,
Sunshine feels warm, bring crystal clear blue skies,
Beauty can be seen in a sunset like mini rainbows,
Colors paint the sky gracefully as night falls.

Hope

Things have gone from bad to worst,
It's almost like you have been cursed
When hope is alive it guides you through,
Good things that happen just seem too good to be true

Living in frustration
Through pain and aggravation
Brings on complication
In any situation

It's difficult to think straight
Trying to focus and concentrate
Being dragged by excess weight
It's hard to be patient and wait

Energetic on my feet with no slack
Under pressure and not wanting to crack
Positive thoughts will keep me on track
Steer me away from turning into a manic

I know I need to breakaway
From all of the stress, anxiety, and dismay
Something to make me feel better today
While I wait for things to get better someday

Spiritual

What affects the soul

Sacred to the believer of God, his words of truth give strength

Pureness opens oneself, feels sweet, new, and refreshing

Innocence in the shadows that follow behind the light of righteousness

Rediscover the soul through positive influence

Intellectual thoughts move and inspire others into new heights

Theological lessons that will be passed on through eternity

Uplifting moments of praise that energize a weak spirit

Advise and preach goodness to those around you

Laudability for giving and sharing in times of need

Best of Book 3:

In Memory of Nancy

I Remember When

I was little and you got me my first bike,
I was so excited, you got it for me
knowing you couldn't afford it.

You would get mad at me when
I said I couldn't do something and to
you that was unacceptable.

We used to go for long walks to get were we had to go when we didn't have money
to catch the bus- that didn't seem to bother you.

I got my first summer job at 14,
you were so happy and made sure that I
got to work on time everyday.

We used to stay up late
watching comedy shows, we
would laugh so hard till we cried.

I would fall and get hurt while playing outside,
I would be in so much pain and you try your best to sooth me and make the pain go away.

How mad and upset you were when you found out I was pregnant, I didn't think you would be there for me but you were.

It was days before you passed away, I knew you weren't feeling your best- you wouldn't tell me why because you didn't want me to worry.

For You I Will

I will do my best in
everything I do each day,

Tell your grandson
how good you were to him,

Remember our close and special
mother-daughter bond we had,

Treasure the lessons that
we taught each other,

Hold my head up when
things take a turn for the worst,

Enjoy myself and be thankful
for what I have in my life,

Think decisions through more carefully
and take my time when needed,

Take advantage of opportunities that come along that can make me a better person,

Not let anyone tell me that I can't do
anything I put my mind to,

Carry on as long as I can until
we meet each again.

This isn't goodbye

To that special someone who was called home to be with The Lord,
They are now is in a safe and better place

I never thought I would lose you
at a point in my life, when I needed you the most,
While going through changes and new events
I looked forward to you being there every step of the way,
just as you have been there for me in the past.
I looked forward to your advice, guidance,
Words of encouragement and praise.
The times when you believed in me
when no one else did made me feel
Good and special, this is something that I'll
always remember about you.
Now all of these things are memories,
Memories I think of to get me through the day or
Through difficult times faced alone.
Our times of struggle and happiness,
all the good times and laughs we shared.
Not only do I look back for strength,
At the same time it inspires me to do better.
I will never forget what a kind, loving and
supportive person you were.
I can feel your presence at places we have been together.
My only hope now is that you will continue to watch over me,
As you did when you here, my guardian angel.
A part of you will always be with me,
a warm place in my heart.
There's no point in saying goodbye because
one day I will see you again,
greeting me at the gates of heaven…

May you forever rest in peace.

N.A.N.C.Y

No one in the world like her, unique, special

A loving, warm, unforgettable individual

Natural and pure in her own way

Caring when others needed help

Youthful at heart with a bright spirit

This never came across my mind
(Haiku)

I never thought that
I would spend the rest of my
life without you here.

November 2nd 2005

My Wednesday started off as usual,
rolling out of bed in the morning,
getting up and heading to work.

Each morning I drive by the brown
house, always noticing how dark and
quiet it looks. I always have the feeling
of wanting to go back to bed and go
to sleep because I knew who lived there;
my mom- the home away from home.

I got to work and I could feel something
wasn't right. I knew mother wasn't feeling
her best so I knew to call her when she got
up later that morning. Unfortunately I never
got to make that call.

All of the sudden within a matter of a few
short hours I got a phone call saying something
was wrong. I had to ride over to mother's house, but I kept thinking why? They
wouldn't tell me over the phone- what's going on? The ride to mother's house
seemed so long this morning for some reason- time was trying to prepare me for the
worst.

I finally got to my mother's house-
an awful and uncomfortable scene.
Why are there so many police cars here?
Why are there so many officers standing in the yard?

Where is my mother- I want to see her!
The worst news of my life was waiting for me,
At this point I'm demanding answers
but who do I talk to? Then out of no where a
detective walks up to me- he wants to know some answers to questions he has but
the first thing he said was "I'm sorry for your loss."

"Oh no!"
"No!"
"No- you can't tell me that!"
"She's supposed to be here!"

I can't hold any tears-
I can't think straight-

I lost it- right there in the open!
I didn't have the strength nor
could I even try to stand on my feet.

I'm sitting in the back of a police car-
crying and screaming-
The detective is the last person I want
to look at after hearing such devastating news! I wanted to be left alone!
Don't ask me questions about her!
I'm supposed to answer questions after literally
having all of my strength torn and
drained away from my heart!

Hell- I have questions of my own!
What happen to her? Where did you take her?
How much longer till all of these damn cops
will get off the lawn, out of the house, and just
go the hell away?

"She's at the hospital- she was just pronounced dead."

"I want to go see her- take me to her!" I thought. Riding over to the hospital I
thought the storm was over- but yet everyone didn't know what happened.
Everyone didn't know who God took that morning.
I thought I was in so much pain- I was paralyzed! How could I tell my grandmother
her youngest daughter was gone?

I get to the hospital and all I want to see is my mother. It feels like so much time has
gone by and I haven't seen her yet- then a few doctors and nurses come asking me
more questions- I just want to see her for goodness sake!

I finally get to her and I just realized at the point this will be one of the last times I'll
see her. She looked as if she was sleeping- I kept thinking come on mommy, wake
up, please, wake up? I knew deep down she wasn't.
She was long gone.

I held her hand for as long as I could
and just looked at her, as I had my last
silent cry with her. I spoke to her.

I let her know that I will remember everything
you told me and that I will try and do my best
to make us **both** happy.

She wanted me to remember that she was
happy- for the longest time when we talked
about that it didn't make sense, until I saw
her motionless in the bed. I think at this point
of the day that was the only peaceful sight I had.

My heart has been ripped out of my chest!
A void was created and nothing can fill it.
My body is aching and sore-
I know I can't do anything
for the rest of the day-
It was dark in that room but it was so
sunny when I walked outside of the hospital.

A new chapter in my life just started
but now I had to figure out where to
go from here and most of all I was starting
on a new journey- alone.

Some Days…

I'm still in shock over
the fact that you passed away
so suddenly,

I can't think straight on
solving things that you used to
help me with,

I try to be happy and have fun
but it just doesn't
feel the same,

It's been more difficult
to go on doing
my normal daily routines,

I can't stand being around those
who knew you-their memories
of you hurt too much,

I believe you're trying to communicate
to me through my dreams or
by way of nature,

I can't look at a picture of you
because it tends to
reopen unhealed wounds,

Some days, you're all I think about.

Your Grandson Willie

The youngest family member who had
a hard time saying goodbye,
Though he was just 16 months old
he knew he lost his close and
best friend- grandma.
Not to long after grandma passed on,
he would run through the house
looking for his friend like they were
playing a game of hide and go seek
or peek-a-boo.
He knows grandma played with him often.
Willie would get very frustrated when
he didn't find his friend.
He would stand at the bottom of the
stair case yelling and talking as if
his friend was at the top of the stairs
listening to him. He would pause…
Waiting for a response-
only to get frustrated once again.
He looks at pictures of you-
he looks at them very closely.
I guess he tries to get in the picture-literary,
just to be with his friend.
When we visit your resting place he tends
to get very happy while playing with flowers
and running around in the open space.
I think he knows his friend is their- he gets mad
when it's time to go home,
just like when he was at grandma's house.

The root of my sadness
(Haiku)

Though we were very
close some memories slowly
start to fade away.

So What's Next?

What I have done in my first year without you
will reflect on my future and what I plan to do.

I still haven't figured out all details of the plan
yet I know that God will help me understand.

How far will I go and where will be a surprise
but when I succeed that will be my prize.

The future is impossible to predict and see
but I know plenty will be there for me.

I'll end up making choices- wrong or right
making things appear in a brighter light.

I can say that I'm not afraid of dying,
but more like being afraid of not living.

So I must take opportunity as it comes around
using my new sense of confidence I've found.

In a way this will still be exciting and new
on my way to making a dream come true.

I'm filled with anxiety-my mind perplexed
wondering and asking myself: so what's next?

Now Showing: The One Woman Show

I found comfort doing something new

A way to express myself and be true,

I just got started before you passed away

So I didn't get to tell you all I wanted to say,

I guess that's okay because you'll still know

While being up above and watching me grow,

I hope you'll be happy with what I'm doing

Just being in line with dreams I'm pursuing,

I know I'll have support in things I do

It meant more to me when it came from you,

I see myself as the main character in the show

You'll be watching me to see how far I can go.

The Emotion of the Year
(Haiku)

I think I have been
more angry in the last year
than ever before.

Starting to Slip Away

The month of October
has been hard for me,
It's a reminder when
you started to slip away…

Slowly your body was
shutting down on you,
It seemed as if
you had no control.

It made my heart ache-
I felt so bad because
something was bothering
you and I didn't know
what it was.

I was so scared the night
I took you to the E.R.
but nothing happened-
you didn't get the relief
you were seeking.

I helped you as much as I could
but I got so stressed, depressed,
and confused. I put everything
on the back burner-you were my
main concern. I was baffled…

I couldn't understand and it
made me have difficulty thinking-
I would pray and hope that
you would feel better- yet
it's weird because you were
never sick- you just complained
of headaches, but I couldn't get
you to eat and I notice you didn't
have as much strength as you
usually would have.

While traveling back and forth
from work to your place I watched
you very closely, but God knew there
was only so much I could do, even
though I tried my best I thought I failed.

I wondered if I should
have done something
that I didn't- I guess
that wasn't in God's plan.

But in someway I think
he was preparing to take you
and relieve you of your discomfort-
that alone was to much for
both you and I to bare.

Cleaning Out Mom's House

The difficulty was at an all time high
Going through belongings- saying goodbye,

Exhausted- trying to adjust to change
It's not easy since it feels so strange,

I can't believe I have to do this
Getting rid of things from some one I'll miss,

Lord knows this won't be easy
Just the thought makes my stomach queasy,

Every time I go to pick something up it hurts
From furniture, jewelry, shoes and shirts,

The house empty with no life or breathing soul
It's like looking into a deep black hole,

This was how a chapter in my life began
With nothing in place- not even 1 plan,

Standing in the front yard looking at the house
Wiping tears away with sleeves of my blouse,

The moment comes where I have to move on
Without my mother because she is gone.

Holding On
(Haiku)

All I can do is
remember you as you were
as long as I can.

That's kind of Spooky...

From time to time I still get very
cautious about what decisions
I make-

Not just because it was what we
talked about or that you told
me you didn't want me doing it-

(Of course you wouldn't let me off the hook easy)

I feel a presence watching over my
shoulder sometimes, then I get the feeling
that I can make a clear decision-

I still have a fear that if it's not the right
decision that I will suffer the consequences-

Even though your not physically here-
if I do something wrong-
my consequences may not just be from God...

That's like saying you really haven't gone anywhere-

To me that's kind of spooky...

July 28th 1982
(Haiku)

The day I was born
has a new meaning to me
that's close to my heart.

A Loving Memory Keepsake

Something I made that I carry always,

Filled with memories, thoughts, special days,

It's a project that I'm always adding to,

By way of things that remind me of you,

It keeps you deep within my soul and heart,

Pictures and poems- my memento of fine art,

It's filled with so much more than I can say,

It gives me strength each and everyday.

Simply Saying Thanks

I really did appreciate everything you did for me, and I hope you felt the same way too. Well we would argue a lot and times I know you felt unappreciated. My actions may not have always reflected that- so I'm sorry if I made you feel bad, mad, or sad- yet I think you knew how much I really was grateful for what you did. I may not have said it in words but I showed it in actions. This is just my way of simply saying thanks.

Best of Book 2:

Trials and Tribulations of Depression: Haiku, Quotes, and Thoughts from the Soul

Finding myself will
take lots of time and patience
which will help me grow.

Why was the time now
to break away from this shell
that kept me enclosed?

I don't think I will
be completely cured from this
illness but I'll live.

Starting a new path
through living each day better
than the day before.

Looking back into
the past made me realize I
took things way to far.

Each day I hope to
feel a little bit better
one day at a time.

Without believing
things never getting better
will not have a chance.

Very slowly I'm
starting to find my way through
the hurt and torment.

My body begins
to lift from a long slumber
that kept me captive.

It's not easy
to shake off negative vibes
that became a shadow

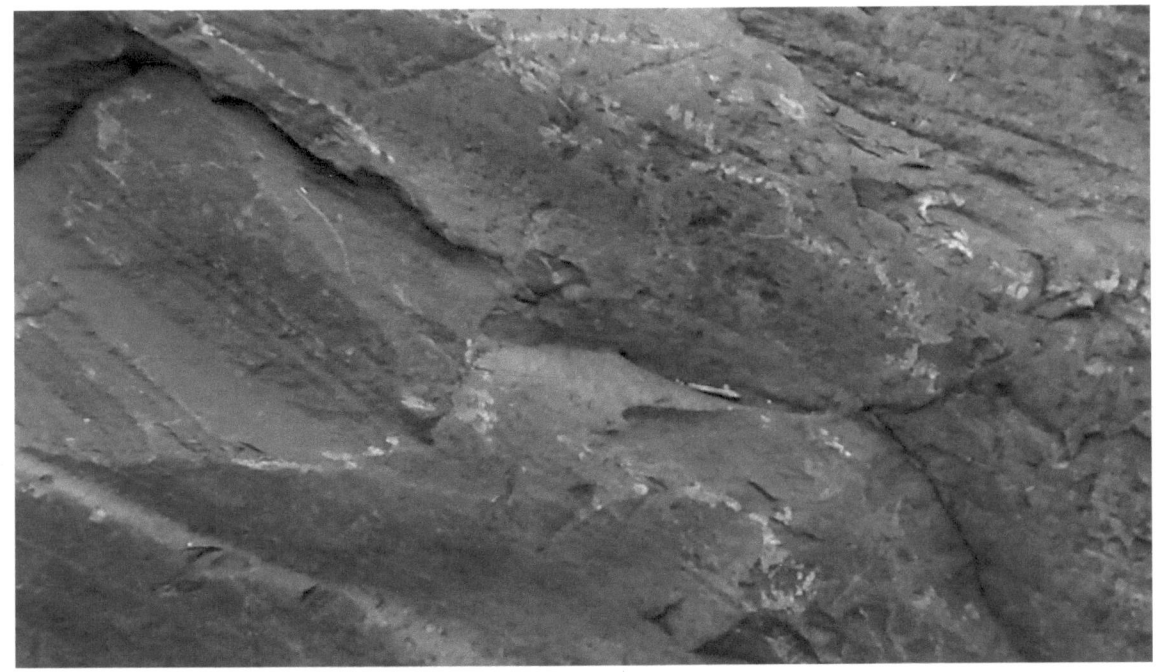

A daily struggle
losing focus on ones faith
is like losing strength.

New Pieces of Poetry

Why do I?

Why do I constantly feel angry and irritated?

Why do I not have the strength to laugh but enough energy to cry?

Why do I bother trying to make others comfortable or happy when I can never please myself?

Why do I feel like the sunlight is too much to bare?

Why do I let my mind wonder and drown into negative thoughts?

Why do I feel that people are hurting me when they are trying to help me?

Why do I cry for no reason?

Why do I feel so hopeless and why does that not bother me?

Why do I have thoughts of not wanting to live?

Why do I look at others and automatically think they are better than me?

Why do I feel tired and weak even though I didn't do any work?

Why do I feel better when I'm left alone?

Why do I let other people's comments get to me?

Why do I lie to myself day after day?

Why do I think that putting myself down often is normal?

Why do I often wish I lived another life being another person yet I don't want to live at all?

Why do I feel that I don't deserve anything?

Why do I feel guilty over something that hasn't happen yet?

Why do I have dozens of questions going through my mind with no answers or solutions?

Mirror, Mirror

I look into the mirror and what do I see?

A person who does not represent me.

I can look into the eyes and see a part of my soul,

That's tired and drained because depression has taken its toll.

To others these eyes may look normal and okay,

But that's something that no one else can say.

I see a person who is worn out and beginning to fade away,

Because life has gotten confusing and worthless with each passing day.

In just seconds I get a glimpse of someone I can't bare,

Sadness and shame follows my despair.

Funny is to Laugh

Jokes that are supposed to be funny,

well to me they are not.

I have to put on an act and a smile,

for those that surround me.

I wonder what actually makes them laugh?

Did I miss something? Or did it miss me?

Road Rage

I can't stand driving behind someone who is going to slow for me,

I feel like I'm being held behind because I have a place I need to be.

My impatience will make me dodge and weave through traffic,

I'm going so fast filled with fury not thinking to be careful before causing havoc.

Not wanting to look or see other cars in my way,

I could care less how they see me flying up the street or what they have to say.

I'm not thinking about getting caught for speeding,

Simply because I ignore the speedometer in my car that I should be reading.

I should know to be more careful driving on the road before it's too late,

But I don't think about that while being in a tired, rundown, irritated mental state.

Sunny Days

There are days were I can't stand looking at the sunlight.

It bothers me because it doesn't seem right.

The sight is supposed to be calm, plentiful, and beautiful.

I would rather it be cloudy and dreary, to most this may sound dreadful.

I remember when along time ago when I was very young,

Seeing the sunrise marking a new day has begun.

The colors used to be soothing, comfy, and warm

Just like when the sun reappears following an afternoon storm.

I don't know what happened since then because I don't see that anymore,

The sight of day just reminds me that living is just a chore.

Not knowing or understanding what changes have come over me,

Even on the brightest days I sense darkness and that's what I see.

Happy One Minute, Crabby the Next

I can be happy
for no apparent reason
which leads to sadness.

Understanding

Constant worry of what is going on in the world around me,

Not understanding reality versus false thoughts.

Hardly trying to comprehend what is said during conversation,

Not understanding the message that I should have picked up.

At the end of the day I feel drained from frustration and confusion,

Not understanding the thought of making it through the day and knowing it's a blessing.

I hardly think about the future and what my expectations are,

Not understanding the importance of life and it's affects on others.

Thinking clearly is something that just can not be done,

Not understanding how to organize my thoughts.

To be left alone during the day is what I want more than anything,

Not understanding how others perceive me or my actions.

Questions are always on my mind about why I am living,

Not understanding the answers that come in the form of actions.

A Rainy Day

Rainy days remind me of

lost feelings and thoughts

that fall out of place and collect

themselves later on.

Related thoughts grow

into a puddle and with a splash in which

they make themselves visible.

But if you don't act on them

or let them sit to long

they begin to dissipate or disappear

into a mind that is lost.

Wasted energy, wasted fuel

because the mind is mentally disfigured

it mistakes elements that should nurture

as elements acidic to the life line of the mind.

A Jungle

The human mind can
go wild at anytime
without a warning.

Who are you dad?

A million and one questions need to be answered…
Yet it seems there's no time for explanation-
When I would ask mom about you she would give mixed emotions;
Was she hurting from something in the past?
Or was she sad and angry that you weren't there to support your daughter?
There was love between mom and you wasn't there?
What happened?
Where did you go and run off to?
What was more important than helping support your child?
There are so many things you missed out on over the last 25 years-
One of the most important things was the birth of your grandson,
I wonder what am I supposed to tell him about his grandfather when he's older?
I also go on day to day with mixed emotions,
I'm angry because you weren't there,
sad and confused because I don't know who you are-
Wondering what it would be like to have a father-period.
What would we have done together?
What lessons would you have taught me?
Would I have had siblings instead of being an only child?
Do I look like you or have any of your features?
All of these years I have been jealous of others who have what I wanted-
Those who have what I wish I had-
To say the words "my father" in the same sentence doesn't make sense to me-
It feels unnatural.
I am happy to have my son and know that he has a good father-
I feel as if I was able to give him something I wanted for years-
Something I felt bad about, cried about, and wondered about for a long time.
If you were to walk into my life today- I'm not sure I would want you here…
You weren't here for over 20 years so why would I want to see you now?

Haunted Nightmare

A traumatic event-
my worst nightmare that came true that
continues to haunt me till this day
I remember it like it was yesterday-
the night was clear, warm, with a light breeze in the air
but for some reason I couldn't sleep- I was awake into the wee hours of the morning

Trying to relax in bed I hear footsteps approaching the back porch-
kicking and banging- kicking and banging
vibrations getting stronger and louder by the minute
Quickly I sat up in bed as I realized there was another person in the house-
my heart started racing- my pulse was stuck in my throat
I felt like I couldn't swallow- all I could do was sit still and pray…

Heavy footsteps crept up the stairs in the darkness of the hall-
a tall black figure came closer to my bedroom door and
all I could focus on was what this tall dark figure had in it's hand…
The heavy footsteps stopped into my room-
the light switch was cut on and to my surprise the robber spoke to me…
"Just lay there-don't say a word!" in a deep threatening voice with a
gun pointed to my head…

At that moment I stopped breathing-
I froze as my heart began beating harder and faster
I was afraid to even take a breathe- wondering if that would provoke him to shoot…
A long pause follows as I'm just waiting-
waiting to see the flash from the gun once the trigger is pulled
waiting to see if a single bullet was going to end my life
all I could think about was why should I have die at 13?
why this way? what did I do to deserve this moment?

I just wanted this moment to be over!
I just want him to go away and leave me alone…
I'm hoping my mother stays asleep- I don't even want to think about him doing
something to her…

I sat in shock and in silence-
watching him salvage through my belongings
taking change and anything of value…

He ran across the hall to my mother's room and
continued on his hunt for what he could claim as his-
quietly walking through her room and snatching her purse…

With his hands full of valuables and his weapon-
he turns the light out- pointing the gun at me several times,
enough to leave freeze frame photos in my mind as the
heavy footsteps crept back to the top of the stairs-
he looks at me once more in the dark-points his gun as if he was hesitating to pull
the trigger and traveled down the steps…

I sat in my bed in a daze-
I'm still alive- is this a dream? I'm awake right?
No- maybe it's a nightmare or a bad dream- if so then why am I already awake?
My eyes continue to blink quickly as I look down at myself-
Did this just happen?

One of my worst fears haunted me in my sleep-
as many dreams as I have had about this scenario you would think it should be no
surprise, but in a way it reminds me of death…

You see it over and over again and nothing can prepare you for it-
at the same time the idea or that thought will find a way to haunt you…

Hang in There

So exhausted I feel like doing nothing
and I can't sit still to finish anything

I have a million things to do; time- there's never enough
while trying to think under pressure it becomes very rough

So what is this feeling that I'm trying to fight?
Confusion? Frustration? I just don't feel right

Wondering what's going on inside
as I try to find someone to confide

I look at things around me but it doesn't seem real
Maybe that's affecting how I truly feel

They say you should talk about problems to help you feel good
My fear is if I try I'll be misunderstood

I don't understand why I'm feeling this way
The least I can do for the moment is hang on and pray

www.therrinpoetry.com

Inspirational Published Works by Author Tanisha L. Herrin

Proceeds from *Inspire the Heart, Inspire the Mind, Inspire the Spirit* and *In Memory of Nancy*
Benefit the Nancy A. Herrin Foundation Inc.
www.nancyherrinfoundation.org

72 Pgs.

84 Pgs.

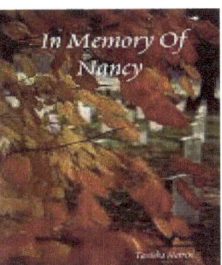
64 Pgs

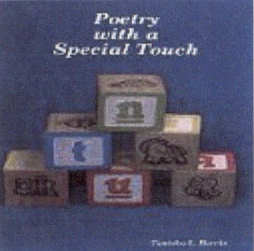
45 Pgs

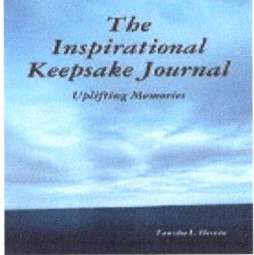
215 Pgs

www.ingramcontent.com/pod-product-compliance
Lightning Source LLC
Chambersburg PA
CBHW041152290426
44108CB00002B/44